NAMIBIA
in Pictures

Tom Streissguth

Twenty-First Century Books

Contents

Twenty-First Century Books
A division of Lerner Publishing Group, Inc.
241 First Avenue North
Minneapolis, MN 55401 U.S.A.

Website address: www.lernerbooks.com

Library of Congress Cataloging-in-Publication Data

Streissguth, Thomas, 1958–
    Namibia in pictures / by Tom Streissguth.
        p. cm. – (Visual geography series)
    Includes bibliographical references and index.
    ISBN 978-0-8225-8574-9 (lib. bdg. : alk. paper)
    1. Namibia—Juvenile literature. 2. Namibia–Pictorial works–Juvenile literature. I. Title.
DT1519.S77 2009
    968.81—dc22   2007040991

4651

Manufactured in the United States of America
1 2 3 4 5 6 - BP - 14 13 12 11 10 09

INTRODUCTION

Unlike many African countries, the Republic of Namibia has managed a peaceful transition from colony to independent nation. One of the world's youngest countries, it gained independence in 1990, after a century as a colonial possession of Germany and then South Africa. Since independence, Namibia has enjoyed steady economic growth and one of the highest per capita (per person) incomes in Africa.

Modern Namibia is a complex patchwork of ethnic groups, languages, and cultural traditions. The region has been subject to waves of settlement by outsiders for millennia. The San people, who speak a Khoisan language, are the oldest inhabitants of desert regions in southern and eastern Namibia. Bantu speakers, who originally came from central Africa, live in tightly knit farming and ranching communities throughout the nation. Europeans who colonized southern Africa, in particular the Germans, have left their mark on Namibia's cities and towns.

After independence, Namibia adopted a new constitution. It guides the country in lawmaking and in holding regular democratic elections. The country began a program of land reform, in which landowners were encouraged to voluntarily sell their acreages to those seeking to establish themselves as independent farmers and ranchers. The goal is to spread landownership across a broader section of the population, both in economic terms and in ethnic background. In addition, Namibia has declared English as the official language. This act was an attempt to promote investment and closer ties to foreign nations, since English is the commonly accepted language of commerce. Still, a very small percentage of the population actually speaks English.

The country has growing pains. The distribution of land is still unequal. Most productive land is still in the hands of white Namibians, who are a small segment of the population. Unemployment is high, and many neighborhoods have limited public services. In addition, Namibia has some environmental challenges. Much of the land is desert, and

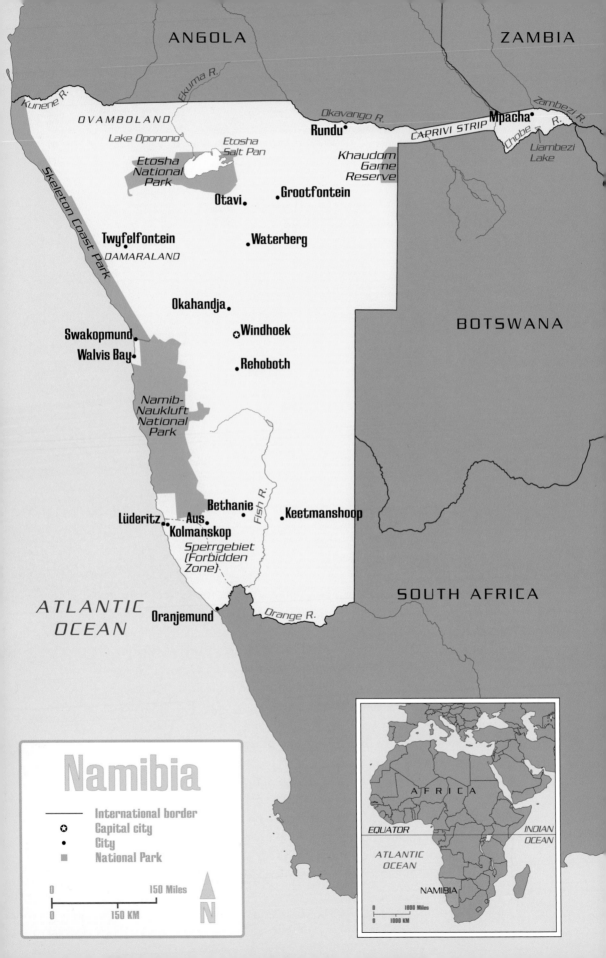

water supplies are scarce. Its wildlife and flora are under pressure from tourism and development. There are also problems in public health. Like many African nations, Namibia has a high rate of disease, including malaria and AIDS (acquired immunodeficiency syndrome).

Nevertheless, Namibia has abundant natural resources. The country is rich in minerals. Its beautiful desert landscapes, national parks, and wildlife draw more tourists every year. Namibia has also achieved political stability. The constitution passed at independence guarantees every citizen above the age of eighteen the right to vote. Political parties cooperate in representing the many ethnic groups that populate the country.

Namibia has also kept peace with its neighbors since independence. It has managed this feat despite a violent history of colonization by South Africa and a civil war in nearby Angola. With careful preservation of resources and continued peace among its different ethnic groups, the country's future looks bright and prosperous.

THE LAND

The Republic of Namibia is a large, arid, and sparsely populated nation in southwestern Africa. Its borders extend about 820 miles (1,320 kilometers) from north to south and 380 miles (612 km) from east to west. Its neighbors are South Africa to the south, Botswana to the east, and Angola and Zambia to the north. The Atlantic Ocean forms a long coastline to the west. Namibia's total area is 318,696 square miles (825,418 sq. km), making it about half the size of the state of Alaska.

Topography

Namibia's landscape divides roughly into four major regions: the Namib Desert in the west, the Central Plateau in the center, the Kalahari Desert in the east, and the Bushveld in the northeast.

The Namib Desert runs along the coast of the Atlantic Ocean, from the Orange River in the south to the border with Angola in the north. Flat gravel plains support sparse vegetation, mostly lichens and scrub that draw moisture from underground springs and morning fogs.

The Huns Mountains rise in the far south, north of the Orange River and the border with South Africa. The northern reaches of the Namib Desert include the barren Skeleton Coast and the Kaokoveld, a rugged, harsh desert within the Namib. Also within the desert is the Namib Sand Sea, a vast expanse of orange red sand dunes. Southwesterly winds blowing inland shape and propel the dunes across the landscape.

The Escarpment is a series of hills and ridges rising at the eastern edge of the Namib Desert. Fog and light rainfall arrive with clouds moving across the coast. The clouds condense and drop precipitation as the terrain rises to more than 6,500 feet (1,981 meters). Shrubs, hardy grasses, and acacia trees thrive in the Escarpment. It is also home to a great variety of insects, birds, and reptiles.

The Central Plateau lies at Namibia's highest elevations, between 2,950 and 6,235 feet (900 and 1,900 m) above sea level. This region includes the highest point in Namibia, Königstein. It rises 8,550 feet (2,606 m) in the Brandberg Mountains. Positioned between inhospitable

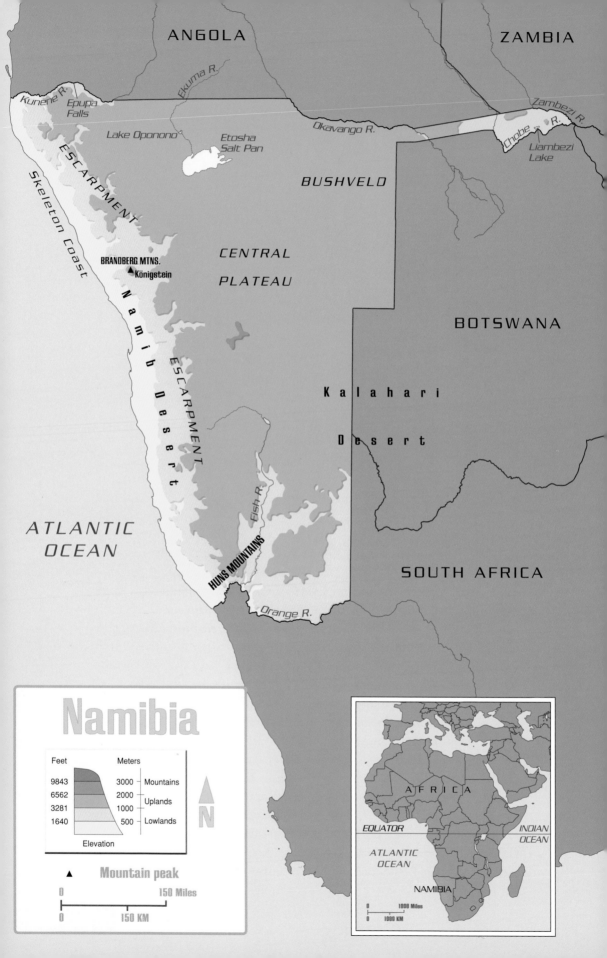

deserts, the Central Plateau is home to a majority of the population and is also the site of the capital city of Windhoek. With fertile land well suited to grazing and some crop growing, the Central Plateau supports agriculture as well as industry.

The Kalahari Desert covers large areas of eastern Namibia, western Botswana, and northern South Africa. The desert is the largest in southern Africa. It contains large regions of scrub plains, along with scattered fertile oases watered by underground springs. Some stretches of the Kalahari receive moderate rainfall in the winter, allowing several thousand species of hardy desert plants known as succulents to thrive. Inselbergs ("island mountains" in German) are isolated peaks that rise from the desert floor. Animal and plant species thrive on the slightly cooler slopes of the peaks.

Namibia's Skeleton Coast was named for the bones of the many people whose bodies washed up on these Atlantic shores. Even survivors of shipwrecks soon died of thirst and exposure to the sun. Namibia's shoreline also holds the remains of many wrecked ships. Some are surrounded by sand dunes.

The Bushveld region of northeastern Namibia stretches from the Angolan border eastward through the narrow Caprivi Strip, a finger of land linking Namibia to Zambia. The eastern limit of the Caprivi Strip lies near but does not touch the border of Zimbabwe. Rainfall in the Bushveld is higher in this area than anywhere else in Namibia. The sandy soil of this savanna (grassland), or veld, region is difficult to farm, however. The most important economic activity is herding livestock. The Etosha Salt Pan is a salt flat that is transformed into a lake during the rainy season, attracting a great variety of birds and mammals. The area has been protected as the Etosha National Park.

Rivers and Lakes

Few perennial (year-round) rivers flow in Namibia. Those that do provide an essential source of water for the country's limited farming. In many areas, drinking water is scarce as well. A drought that has lasted for years has made the country even drier, and water has become the subject of local and international disputes.

The Okavango River, the largest river of northern Namibia, has its source in Angola. It forms part of the border between Namibia and Angola before flowing eastward into Botswana, where it eventually dries up in a salt marsh. Namibia and Botswana both have a claim to the river's waters. Suffering from drought, Namibia has diverted some of the Okavango's flow for irrigation. Angola, Namibia, and Botswana signed an agreement in 1994 to set up a commission to deal with water rights on the Okavango River.

The Kunene River also flows from Angola but turns westward and empties into the Atlantic Ocean. A series of rapids and the 115-foot (35 m) drop known as Epupa Falls lie along this waterway. The Kunene and its small tributaries provide a steady source of water for surrounding farms.

The Zambezi River touches the border of Namibia at the eastern limit of the Caprivi Strip. The strip was intended to allow Namibia to link with the Zambezi River, which flows eastward into the Indian Ocean. However, the river proved to be too hazardous for commercial navigation.

The Orange River separates Namibia from South Africa. The river rises in the Drakensberg Mountains of South Africa. It passes the Huns Mountains of southern Namibia and an important diamond mining region before finally emptying into the Atlantic at the border town of Oranjemund.

The Orange River marks the border between South Africa and Namibia.

The wetlands of the northern Bushveld region hold several small lakes and marshes. During rainy seasons, Liambezi Lake floods and drains into the Chobe River, which eventually reaches the Zambezi River. At other times, the lake's water level falls, and the lake is transformed into a reed-lined wetland.

Lake Oponono lies north of the Etosha Salt Pan in northern Namibia. The lake drains into the Ekuma River, which eventually reaches the pan in seasons of moderate to heavy rainfall. The Etosha Salt Pan itself is transformed into a large lake after heavy storms.

Climate

Namibia has an arid, or dry, climate. A cold, north-flowing Atlantic Ocean stream known as the Benguela Current creates an area of low pressure offshore. This prevents rain clouds from moving inland, creating one of the most barren coasts in the world. Inland, most precipitation results from monsoon rains that move westward from the Indian Ocean over the southern third of the African continent from October through April. By the time these clouds reach Namibia, however, they have lost most of their moisture. The northeastern Bushveld region is the wettest area of Namibia, receiving about 16 inches (41 centimeters) of rain per year. In the Kalahari and Namib deserts, rainfall is rare and unpredictable. Moisture that does reach the ground quickly evaporates in the heat, leaving very little excess to reach underground springs. The deserts can go for several years without any rain whatsoever.

The Central Plateau has extremes of temperature, reaching 104°F (40°C) in the summer (December through March in Namibia, since it is in the Southern Hemisphere). During the winter months, from June to September, night temperatures can dip below freezing. In Windhoek average temperatures during the winter are 55°F (13°C), while the summers average about 74°F (23°C). The temperatures are moderate in the north, ranging from 86°F (30°C) in summers down to 50°F (10°C) in winter.

Natural Resources

Namibia has limited land for farming but is rich in mineral resources. The diamond fields of southern Namibia produce gemstones that are cut, polished, and sold around the world. Namibia also has deposits of gold, copper, uranium, lead, zinc, salt, coal, cadmium, lithium, coal, and iron ore.

The cold Benguela Current is a habitat for many species of edible fish. Coastal fishing is an important source of income in port cities such as Walvis Bay and Lüderitz. Geologists have also explored offshore

These **rough diamonds** were mined in Namibia. Go to www.vgsbooks.com for links to more information about diamond and other types of mining in Namibia.

DIAMONDS—KEEP OUT!

In April 1908, railway laborer Zachariah Lewala was walking near Kolmanskop, in the southwestern part of modern Namibia. He stumbled on a rough stone with smooth sides. He had already worked in the diamond fields at Kimberly, in modern South Africa, and he recognized this stone as a rough diamond.

Soon a diamond rush was on. The German colonial government established the Sperrgebiet, or "forbidden zone," around Kolmanskop. The German government didn't want anyone taking any of the precious stones. The Sperrgebiet covers about 10,000 square miles (26,000 sq. km) and extends 62 miles (100 km) inland from the Atlantic coast. Within the Sperrgebiet, or National Diamond Area, many diamonds still lie on or near the surface. All visitors and tourists are banned from this rich mining area. It is illegal to trespass or even stop in this area while in a car. Armed patrols promptly show any violators the way out.

for natural gas and oil, although no deposits have yet been exploited. The seabed does hold offshore gemstone deposits, and offshore diamond mining takes place along the coast of southern Namibia.

Namibia's great diversity of animal and plant life is one of its most valuable resources. Large mammals are protected from hunting in a series of national parks, which draw visitors from all over the world.

○ Flora and Fauna

The varied flora and fauna of Namibia have adapted to several different types of land and climate. Desert vegetation, such as lichens and succulents, survive by storing water. They get their water from rainfall, underground springs, or fog that rolls in from the coast in the morning. In the north, the mopane tree provides a reliable source of firewood. Large fig and baobab trees also thrive in this zone. In the southern region are aloe plants, leadwood trees, and the kokerboom. The light, spongy wood of the kokerboom has long been used to make containers for arrows, giving this plant the nickname of quiver tree.

Large mammal species native to Namibia include lions, giraffes, black rhinos, leopards, impalas, elephants, and antelopes. Lions hunt the plains and deserts, preying on permanent populations such as the colonies of seals that inhabit the coast. One of the largest game reserves in the world, the Etosha National Park, covers a salt pan that fills with water during heavy rain. The temporary lake that is created and the marshy land that surrounds it host abundant bird and plant life. Elephants that inhabit Namibia have adapted to desert conditions. They roam rivers and streambeds in search of food and are capable of going several days without water. The deserts of Namibia are also

SMELLY HOODIA

One of the world's more repulsive plants, the hoodia, grows abundantly in Namibia. Whenever it rains, the hoodia sends out purple blooms that smell like rotten meat. The smell brings flies, which drink the plant's sap and then lay their eggs in the blooms. The flies then carry away the plant's pollen, spreading the hoodia to new ground.

Two **giraffes** drink from a river at the Etosha National Park.

THE WILD HORSES OF AUS

A small group of wild horses *(above)* survives in the rugged countryside around the town of Aus in west central Namibia. The horses may be descended from those that arrived with German cavalry (horse-mounted soldiers) in the early twentieth century. They also may be descended from animals that escaped from nearby ranches decades ago. The horses of Aus are the last desert-dwelling wild horses in the world.

home to brown hyenas, meerkats (mongooses), the shovel-snouted lizard, and a snake known as the sidewinder. The golden mole is a blind creature that lives in small air pockets underneath the surface of sand dunes.

◉ Environmental Issues

Sparsely populated, Namibia has escaped many of the urban problems—overcrowding, air pollution, and loss of wildlife habitat—that are common throughout Africa. But the country still faces serious environmental issues. A long-lasting drought, as well as human activities, has led to desertification (changing into desert) of the savanna. Grazing sheep and cattle destroy large swaths of the natural landscape. When plants are lost, the soil is less able to hold moisture and erodes during the rare rainfalls that do occur. The land is also affected by new development, such as roads, homes, tourist facilities, and industrial plants.

In Namibia, land use tends to aggravate environmental problems. Large farms often crowd out smaller ones, forcing some herders onto marginal land. Overcrowding results and then soil erosion and desertification. In addition, drought and overuse affect natural springs. The water becomes more saline (salty) and, in some cases, undrinkable and useless for agriculture. To fix the problem, the Namibian government is planning to divert some of the perennial northern rivers to the drier central and southern regions. These projects will cause still more environmental disruption.

Tourism has brought an increasing number of visitors. Many of them come to see the country's wildlife and natural beauty. In some places, heavy foot and vehicle traffic has marked the landscape and driven off wildlife. Poaching (illegal hunting) of large mammals is also a serious problem. It affects elephants, large cats, and rhinoceros. Namibia has set aside many protected areas, where hunting is banned and the impact of human traffic is limited. In addition, Namibia was the first country in the world to include protection of the environment as an article of its constitution.

> Visit www.vgsbooks.com for links to websites with additional information about the environmental issues facing Namibia, as well as what the Namibian people and government are doing to face these issues.

◉ Cities

Most of Namibia's 2 million residents live in urban areas. Bustling streets and marketplaces are common sights in Windhoek as well as in Namibia's many smaller cities.

WINDHOEK, Namibia's capital city, had a population of 233,529, according to the most recent official census, conducted in 2001. (The nation does a census every ten years.) Located in central Namibia, Windhoek was founded on the site of a settlement of the Herero, one of the country's main ethnic groups. The Herero knew the site as Otjomuise, or "place of smoke," for the steamy vapors of local hot springs. The modern city lies among foothills and valleys, where the country's main roads and rail lines meet.

Jonker Afrikaner, a leader of the Oorlam people who arrived from South Africa, founded a settlement in the 1840s and gave the city its modern name. In 1892 Windhoek became the capital of the German colony of Southwest Africa. South Africa occupied the city in 1915, during World War I (1914–1918), and made it the administrative capital. Under South African rule, new roads and schools were built and the city developed some light industry. Upon achieving independence in 1990, Namibia made Windhoek the capital of the new republic.

Windhoek's main street is Independence Avenue. The street is lined with government buildings, hotels, department stores, a zoo, and the Post Street Mall, a shopping district. The Alte Feste, the oldest structure in Windhoek, is an old German fortress built in 1892, that has been turned into the Namibia State Museum.

Independence Avenue is the major street in Windhoek. In 1928 it became the first road in Windhoek to be paved.

RUNDU (population 44,413) is the largest city in northeastern Namibia. It lies on the southern bank of the Okavango River on the border with Angola. The capital of the Kavango region, Rundu was founded in the 1940s as a commercial and transportation city. The city serves as a busy crossing point between the two countries.

WALVIS BAY (population 42,015) is Namibia's main port. It is on the Atlantic coast about 150 miles (242 km) west of Windhoek. The city's name comes from the German term *walfischbai*, or "whale bay." This site provides a deepwater shelter for oceangoing vessels, as well as a feeding ground for whales. The resulting fishing and port activities make it a thriving small commercial center.

The Portuguese explorer Bartolomeu Dias landed at the bay in 1487. The port was annexed (taken over) by the British in the 1840s, occupied by German troops in 1914, and then conquered by the South African army in 1915. Walvis Bay was not officially a part of Namibia until 1994, four years after independence.

REHOBOTH (population 21,300) lies 54 miles (87 km) south of Windhoek. It was once a town of the Nama people, who knew it as !Anis. (The exclamation point stands for a click in the Nama language.) German missionaries arrived in 1845 and renamed the settlement Rehoboth. Basters, or mixed-race settlers, then came up from the Cape Colony to the south in 1868. The Basters established hundreds of ranches in the area and quickly boosted the town's population. Rehoboth is still a center for raising livestock and also has developed a local tourist industry for visitors interested in the history of Namibia.

LÜDERITZ (population 30,000) is a small port on Namibia's southwestern coast. German colonists founded the town in 1883 and started a fishing industry as well as a guano business, in which collected bird droppings are used in fertilizer. Although Walvis Bay is a larger port, Lüderitz still hosts a small fishing fleet. Many of its streets still carry German names from when Namibia was a German colony.

HISTORY AND GOVERNMENT

Namibia has been inhabited since the earliest times of human history. Archaeologists have found stone tools there that date back about two hundred thousand years. Eventually, hunters developed large axes, knives, and other utensils. They mastered fire and developed simple language. Later, they combined wood, bone, and stone to make more complex tools.

About twenty thousand years ago, the San were living in southern Africa. In Namibia, archaeologists have found San stone tools and weapons. They have also uncovered thousands of paintings etched into rocks and the walls of caves. The San were nomads who survived by hunting game and gathering roots and nuts. About fifteen thousand years ago, the San developed the bow and arrow for hunting antelope and other abundant game.

The Nama, also known as the Khoi-Khoi, settled in southern Namibia about two thousand years ago. The Nama and the San speak Khoisan languages. These languages originated in southern Africa

and spread through modern Botswana, Namibia, Angola, and South Africa. The Nama foraged for food and grazed sheep and goats in the fertile valleys along the Orange River. Throughout southern Africa, the first settled farmers were also raising crops at about this time. The Damara, another Khoisan-speaking group, were hunter-gatherers and livestock farmers who moved into central Namibia in about the ninth century A.D.

Meanwhile, Bantu-speaking cattle herders were moving into southern Africa. The Bantu migration took place over many centuries and included many different societies. They introduced new, useful technologies, such as ironworking and gold mining. The first Bantu-speaking migrants to Namibia included the ancestors of the modern Herero and Ovambo peoples.

In southern Africa, Bantu speakers eventually came across Khoisan speakers. The Bantu moved onto grazing lands in modern Botswana and South Africa, forcing some of the Khoisan-speaking groups there to shift west and north into Namibia. The stage was set for centuries of conflict over productive land and pasture in the region.

○ Portuguese Expeditions

European explorers began sailing down the coast of western Africa in the fifteenth century A.D. The Portuguese, like other Europeans at the time, were searching for a new sea route to what they called the East Indies (Southeast Asia). A nimble ship known as the caravel allowed them to maneuver in the tricky winds and currents near the African coast. Portuguese navigators believed there might be a route around the southern tip of Africa that would allow them to reach Asia more quickly than by a difficult land route.

A Portuguese expedition led by Diego Cão reached Namibia in 1486. Cão sailed as far as Cape Cross, about 100 miles (161 km) north of Walvis Bay, and raised a stone cross to mark his progress. Another voyage, led by Bartolomeu Dias, soon followed. In 1487 Dias landed at modern Lüderitz, naming the area Angra Pequena (small cove).

While the Portuguese were settling Angola, to the north, the Dutch landed in South Africa. But Europeans had little interest in exploring Namibia's harsh, waterless deserts. They left stone crosses atop prominent hillsides to mark their passage and continued on to the Cape of Good Hope at the southern tip of Africa.

○ Bantu Settlement

Bantu-speaking peoples known as the Herero arrived in Namibia in the middle of the sixteenth century. The Herero settled along the Kunene River and then spread southward. Seeking grazing land for their cattle, the Herero pushed into the central plains. Armed with iron weapons, they forced the San, who still lived a hunter-gatherer lifestyle, onto less fertile desert areas. A smaller Bantu-speaking group known as the Himba remained in northern Namibia.

In the late 1700s, ships from Europe and the United States stopped at Walvis Bay during storms and to repair their vessels. At this time, Dutch farmers were settling the Cape Colony (part of present-day South Africa) south of the Orange River. Europeans battled the Herero and the San over control of resources and access to fertile land. Many local peoples were taken as slaves to work on Dutch colonial farms. These conflicts forced small groups of Khoisan speakers, known as the Oorlam, to move across the Orange River and northward into present-day Namibia. With guns and horses acquired from the Europeans, the Oorlam lived by raiding local villages and hunting. In small groups led by leaders known as *kaptein*, they also fought the Nama people who had already settled north of the Orange River.

In 1793 the Cape Colony seized control of Walvis Bay, a valuable port. Four years later, when war broke out between the French and the Dutch in Europe, Great Britain seized the bay as well as the Cape Colony. European missionaries began arriving in present-day Namibia in 1805. British, German, and Finnish missionaries established small settlements and converted local peoples to Christianity. In 1811 members of the London Missionary Society, a British group that had originally been working in the Cape Colony, founded the town of Bethanie in southern Namibia.

A ROCKY SHOWER

Scientists believe that a large extraterrestrial body plunged into Earth's atmosphere about 600 million years ago. It broke into pieces, showering present-day southern Namibia with massive chunks of iron and rock. The Gibeon meteorite field is the largest ever discovered. It covers an area 62 by 155 miles (100 by 250 km). The meteorites weigh as much as 20 tons (18 metric tons) each. They have been moved to natural history museums throughout the world. Thirty-three of them decorate a public fountain on Post Street in Windhoek.

This Gibeon meteorite is at a museum in Hawaii. It was discovered in Namibia in 1836.

Conflict and Truce

Fighting soon broke out between the Oorlams and the Nama over their rights to hunting grounds and over tribute (money or goods paid to a ruler) demanded by the Oorlams from the Nama and other groups. Armed with guns brought from the south, the Oorlams proved to be a formidable military enemy. But they also used diplomacy. In 1840 the Nama and the Oorlams reached a truce. The Nama chief Oaseb recognized the Oorlam leader Jonker Afrikaner as the authority over central Namibia. Afrikaner set up his capital in present-day Windhoek. This site attracted missionaries and became a hub of trails and roads across Namibia.

Conflict continued in the central plains between the Oorlam and the Herero, who were pushing southward from their old homeland in northern Namibia. Eventually, the Oorlam prevailed over the Herero as well and collected regular tribute from both the Herero and the Nama.

Meanwhile, German missionaries belonging to the Rhenish Missionary Society were arriving in Namibia. The missions they built—and the services they provided—prompted the Nama to settle nearby and begin building small farms. Traders traveled between the missions, allowing the Nama to obtain European goods, food, tools, and weapons. In 1868 the Basters crossed the Orange River into Namibia and founded the city of Rehoboth. This ethnic group, whose ancestors were both European (mainly Dutch) and African, set up a republic, with elected representatives and a constitution. The Republic of Rehoboth was the first organized state on Namibian territory.

German Southwest Africa

After the death of Jonker Afrikaner in 1861, conflict broke out among the different ethnic groups in Namibia. Colonists from the Cape Colony skirmished with the Nama, the Oorlam, and smaller groups inhabiting southern Namibia. Meanwhile, a European hunter, Charles Andersson, built a post known as Otjimbingwe between Windhoek and the coast. From this spot, Andersson allied with the Herero of the north in battling the Namas. He was mortally wounded during a battle in 1864, while the conflict permanently weakened the Nama.

The violence prompted European settlers and missionaries to ask for protection from the British colonial government of neighboring Cape Colony. At this time, European nations were interested in expanding their African colonies. Great Britain was worried that Germany might decide to colonize Namibia. To head off that possibility, Great Britain annexed (took control of) Walvis Bay in 1878. Great Britain also agreed to several peace treaties with African chiefs in Namibia to bring stability to the region.

German chancellor Otto von Bismarck initially denied his country's colonial interest in Namibia. But he changed his policy in the 1880s, a period when European nations took control of almost all of Africa. In 1883 the German merchant Adolf Lüderitz purchased the coastal town of Angra Pequena from a Nama chief, Joseph Fredericks. Lüderitz renamed this town after himself. In 1884 he convinced the German government to establish the colony of German Southwest Africa.

Adolf Lüderitz

Although the Germans had little hope of developing the remote and arid territory, they sent a few officials to Lüderitz and Otjimbingwe. They offered treaties of protection to the Herero. The Germans encouraged rivalry among the Herero, the Nama, the Oorlams, and other African peoples over land and resources. The Germans hoped to prevent a unified effort to oust the Europeans from the colony. In 1890 Germany and Britain signed the

This photograph of the city of Lüderitz was taken shortly after its purchase from Joseph Fredericks in 1883.

Heligoland-Zanzibar Treaty. The treaty added the Caprivi Strip to the colony of German Southwest Africa. The strip opened a link to the Zambezi River, which led to German colonies in East Africa.

German troops known as Schütztruppe had been arriving in German Southwest Africa to protect German settlers there. The German forces built a fortress in Windhoek in 1890 and fought frequent battles with a Nama group led by Hendrik Witbooi. The German colonial governor, Theodor Leutwein, set up regional centers in Windhoek, Otjimbingwe, and Keetmanshoop. Under his administration, the first railroad in the colony was built between Windhoek and Swakopmund, a coastal port.

In 1894, after several years of conflict, Witbooi signed a treaty with the German colonists. Sporadic fighting between colonists and local black farmers and herders continued, as colonists claimed land that had been used for generations by the Nama and the Herero as pasture. The African herders and nomads were gradually forced into small protected enclaves. Colonists then moved onto the good grazing land and built new towns and missions.

Defeat of the Herero

The Herero of the north had suffered greatly from colonial expansion. A full-scale revolt broke out in 1904. The Herero, led by Samuel Maharero, raided German farms and outposts, killing as many as one hundred settlers. Although Maharero asked Hendrik Witbooi to join the revolt, the Nama leader refused to make any alliances with the ancient enemies of his people.

This illustration from a 1904 edition of a French journal shows the **Herero revolt** against the Germans at Windhoek.

General Lothar von Trotha, appointed the commander in chief of German Southwest Africa in 1904, arrived in June of that year with orders to crush the Herero rebellion. Germany sent fourteen thousand troops to Namibia. They maneuvered the Herero into a full-scale battle at Waterberg on August 11, 1904. The superior German guns and artillery defeated the Herero. After the battle, the Schutztruppe mercilessly hunted down the Herero. They died by the thousands as a result of violence, hunger, and thirst.

To drive the group permanently from German Southwest Africa, German troops poisoned water wells and shot any Herero they saw, even those who had not taken part in the fighting. Surviving Herero were herded into concentration camps. German farmers used them as slave labor and worked many of them to death. More than three-quarters of the Herero population died or fled the colony. Later, von Trotha used the same tactics against the Nama.

Witbooi, meanwhile, had joined the fight, ordering his Nama followers to mount hit-and-run attacks against the German troops. This guerrilla war took place in the Kalahari Desert, where the Nama used their knowledge of the desert to survive and evade capture. Both sides were unable to gain an advantage in the harsh terrain, however, and Witbooi was killed while fighting near Tses in 1905. The conflict ended with treaties known as *Schutzvertrage*, or "protection treaties," in 1907. These agreements allowed the German forces to interfere in conflicts among the African peoples or between whites and blacks in the colony.

Hendrik Witbooi

Settlement by Europeans increased after diamonds were discovered near Lüderitz in 1908. The colonists built new roads and railroads and forced black Namibians onto marginal lands. Germany granted the colony its own administration and lawmaking body at about this time.

At the outbreak of World War I in Europe in 1914, Britain declared war on Germany. In 1915 the Union of South Africa (established in 1910 and ruled by Great Britain) moved troops into German Southwest Africa and occupied the colony. Soon after, the Germans formally surrendered to South Africa at Khorab, near the city of Otavi. By agreements signed after the war, the League of Nations (a group set up to help resolve

South African troops lead German prisoners of war through what was then German Southwest Africa in 1915.

international disputes) gave a mandate to South Africa to administer the colony, renamed South-West Africa. South Africa organized a legislative assembly for white residents of South-West Africa in 1926.

◎ Rule by South Africa

After World War I, thousands of white settlers moved into central Namibia from South Africa. Black African groups were forced into so-called native areas that had generally poor land. These native areas included Bushmanland, Hereroland, and Damaraland. The South African settlers also forced many black people northward to the border region of Angola, a Portuguese colony. Black Africans were employed as inexpensive laborers on farms and to work the mines built by South African companies.

In 1946, after World War II (1939–1945), the United Nations (UN) replaced the League of Nations. The UN asked to oversee South Africa's actions in South-West Africa. Instead, the South African government announced in 1947 that it would directly annex South-West Africa as a new province. It extended its policy of apartheid, or forced separation of black and white Africans into South-West Africa. South Africa also allowed for white representatives from South-West Africa to be in the South African parliament. Throughout the 1950s, South Africa defied UN resolutions that called for autonomy for the black African inhabitants of the province.

By the 1960s, many African colonies were gaining independence. In 1966 the UN formally revoked South Africa's mandate to administer South-West Africa. The UN recognized the name Namibia for the territory in 1968. The name came from a word for "empty plains" in the Khoisan language. The UN formally declared the South African administration in Namibia illegal and called for South Africa to withdraw. Although the UN proposed economic sanctions (restricted trade) against South Africa, these measures were vetoed (voted down) by the members of the UN Security Council.

In the meantime, a guerrilla group of black Africans known as the South West Africa People's Organization (SWAPO) took up arms to fight for independence. SWAPO, based among the Ovambo people of northern Namibia, mounted its first attacks in 1966 from its bases in Zambia. In 1975 SWAPO also began raiding Namibia from the newly independent nation of Angola to the north.

Despite the heavy costs of fighting in Namibia, South Africa remained strongly opposed to Namibian independence. South Africa wanted to protect the wealth that flowed from Namibian diamond mines and trade carried out through Walvis Bay. The conflict grew more complicated when Cuban troops arrived in Angola to take part in a civil war in that country. The Cuban forces allied themselves

TOWNSHIP LIFE

When Namibia was a colony of South Africa, the colonial government imposed apartheid to separate white and black populations. While whites often lived in more affluent areas, urban blacks had to live in townships. These areas near the cities often had limited access to services, such as running water, paved roads, and schools.

Apartheid is no longer legal in Namibia or South Africa, but the townships have survived in both nations. Many still have problems–high unemployment, lack of health facilities and basic sanitation, and contaminated water.

CUBA, ANGOLA, AND THE NAMIBIAN CONFLICT

The struggle for Namibian independence involved one nation quite distant from Africa—Cuba. This island nation in the Caribbean Sea was aligned with the Soviet Union, a military superpower and a rival of the United States. Through the Cuban military, the Soviet Union took part in wars of independence throughout Africa as European countries were surrendering their colonies.

Angola, once a colony of Portugal, won its independence in 1975. Cuba sent soldiers, equipment, and advisers to help the Soviet-allied guerrilla forces known as the Popular Movement for the Liberation of Angola (MPLA). Opposing this group was the National Union for the Total Independence of Angola (UNITA). This group allied with the SWAPO forces in Namibia. In Namibia the South African military found itself fighting not only SWAPO but also the MPLA and its Cuban troops. The fighting took place for more than a decade on both sides of the Angola-Namibia border.

with SWAPO and fought several battles with South African troops in Angola as well as in Namibia.

Plan for Independence

In 1977 the United Nations proposed Resolution 435, or the UN Plan. The plan called for a cease-fire in Namibia and for UN-supervised elections. In the next year, South Africa held elections. But it still sought to keep Namibia under the control of a white-led government, which would remain closely allied with South Africa. SWAPO and other pro-independence groups boycotted the elections in protest of South Africa's continued administration of the country. Meanwhile, South Africa continued a costly war in the northern reaches of Namibia against the SWAPO guerrillas.

In 1982 the UN passed a framework for a future Namibian constitution in the Constitutional Principles. The UN also appointed a commissioner to oversee the transition and administer the country after South Africa withdrew. The United States played an important role in negotiations to implement Resolution 435. The United States sought withdrawal of Cuban troops from Angola. The Cubans were aligned with the Soviet Union (a union of fifteen republics that included Russia). The Soviet Union, in turn, asked for South Africa to withdraw from Namibia.

The negotiations resulted in agreements among the United States, Angola, Cuba, the Soviet Union, SWAPO, and South Africa in late 1988. On April 1 of the next year, Resolution 435 went into effect.

South Africa withdrew its forces from Namibia, except for those at the port of Walvis Bay and the Penguin Islands, a small group of twelve islands lying off the Namibian coast, about 25 miles (40 km) south of Lüderitz. Elections for a constituent assembly were held in November 1989. SWAPO won with 57 percent of the vote. With this election, apartheid in Namibia ended.

The seventy-two-member assembly included members of seven different political parties within Namibia. The assembly adopted the Constitutional Principles passed by the UN in 1982. The new constitution went into effect March 21, 1990, when Namibia formally declared its independence. Sam Nujoma, the leader of SWAPO, was appointed by the Constituent Assembly as the newly independent country's first president.

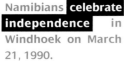
Namibians **celebrate** **independence** in Windhoek on March 21, 1990.

South Africa kept control of Walvis Bay and the Penguin Islands until 1994, when it formally turned over this territory to Namibia. Although conflict arose between SWAPO and the South African army, independent Namibia kept a truce and was able to forge close economic ties with its southern neighbor. When apartheid in South Africa collapsed in 1994, South Africa's new president, Nelson Mandela, assisted Namibia by canceling its debts. Mandela also gave back to Namibia South African property within Namibian borders.

Namibia inherited an infrastructure of roads and railways from the colonial era. Mining and ranching provided a foundation for the economy. Namibia also began to develop a successful tourism industry. However, much of the country's wealth and productive assets were owned by a small class of white landowners and industrialists. Income disparity between blacks and whites contributed to social tensions over the fair division of land and natural resources.

The New Nation

In 1994 Nujoma won a second term as president with more than 75 percent of the popular vote. Although the constitution permitted him only two presidential terms, SWAPO representatives in the assembly amended (changed) the law to permit Nujoma to seek a third term in 1998. The legislature agreed to make the exception as Nujoma had been appointed, not elected, to his first term. Nujoma handily defeated his opponent, Ben Ulenga, in that year.

Shortly after independence, Namibia put into effect a policy of land reform (redistributing the nation's land more fairly among its people). Under the new constitution, land reform was to take place voluntarily. Namibians would not be forced to sell or surrender their land. Instead, the government followed a policy of "willing buyer, willing seller." Few people sold, however. Many people in Namibia believed the policy did not really address the disparity in landownership between wealthy and poor people in Namibia.

Meanwhile, the SWAPO-led government also allied itself with newly independent Angola. Namibia agreed to help in the fight against rebels in southern Angola. Troops from Angola used northern Namibia as a base, while Angolan refugees from the fighting also crossed the border to take shelter from the conflict. By the end of the 1990s, more than thirty thousand refugees were living in camps in northern Namibia. When the fighting died down in Angola, however, most of these refugees returned to their homes.

Trouble was also brewing in the Caprivi Strip. Members of the Lozi people, a small ethnic group of the northeast, were resisting their local governors, members of the Ovambo majority. The Lozi organized to fight for the independence of Caprivi. In August 1999, a small rebel army attacked the airport at the town of Mpacha. The Namibian army—the Namibian Defense Force (NDF)—defeated the rebels, although fighting continued for months. Because the Caprivi region attracts many of Namibia's international visitors, the army has been diligent about holding down rebel activity in the Caprivi Strip.

Current Issues

SWAPO continues to dominate Namibian politics. In the 2004 presidential elections, SWAPO leader Hifikepunye Pohamba won in a landslide, with more than 75 percent of the vote. SWAPO candidates handily defeated their main rival, the Democratic Turnhalle Alliance, for a majority of seats in the legislature. Pohamba, who took office in March 2005, had served under Nujoma as the minister of lands, resettlement, and rehabilitation. In this office, he oversaw the government's land reform policies. Namibians expect Pohamba to carry on the policies of Nujoma, who remains the active president of SWAPO.

Hifikepunye Pohamba *(left)* receives the government's symbols from outgoing president Sam Nujoma during Pohamba's inauguration ceremony.

Namibia maintains good relations with its neighbors, including South Africa. The two countries, however, dispute the exact location of their border along the Orange River. While Namibia marks the border in the middle of the river, South Africa extends it to the northern bank. The dispute has led to problems over fishing rights and use of the river's small islands.

Land reform remains a thorny economic and social issue in Namibia. About half the productive land is claimed by large private commercial farms owned by whites, while many black Namibian farmers scratch out a subsistence living on small plots. To address this inequity, the government is buying some private land for redistribution. The government has also marked off communal (public) lands to be turned into small private farms. A small number of private farms were seized by the government, which then paid the former owners. About two thousand families have been resettled on this productive land.

Foreign investment remains a major pursuit for Namibians. In October 2007, the nation teamed with South Africa to host an international conference for investors. At the conference, the two nations worked to show foreign investors the opportunities in local mining, energy, agriculture, and industry. Among the major potential partners is China, which is poised to become a major economic force in Namibia and throughout Africa.

Visit www.vgsbooks.com for links to websites with additional information about the current events and issues in Namibia. Also find links to information about the ongoing relationship between Namibia and China.

Government

The constitution of Namibia provides for a president, who is elected to a five-year term and serves as head of state and head of government. The president may not serve more than two terms (an exception was made for SWAPO leader Sam Nujoma). The constitution guarantees universal adult suffrage, so all citizens eighteen years old and older may vote in Namibia's elections.

The National Assembly includes seventy-two legislators who are elected to five-year terms. The president may appoint as many as six additional members. These appointed members may debate and propose laws, but they are not permitted to vote.

Namibia is divided into thirteen regions administered by regional councils. Two members of each regional council serve on the National

The National Assembly meets in the **Parliament Building** in Windhoek. The building is open to the public, and citizens can view legislative proceedings from a gallery.

Council, an advisory body that serves as a second house of the legislature. Elected governors administer each of the regions.

The structure of the judicial system remains the same as when Namibia was a province of South Africa. Namibia has thirty local magistrate courts, whose decisions can be reviewed by the High Court. The Supreme Court can hear appeals and decide important cases involving constitutional principles. In some places, community courts decide cases involving civil disputes and traditional customs.

THE PEOPLE

By the official census of 2001, the population of Namibia was 1,826,854. Since then the population has climbed to about 2.1 million. About 43 percent of the population is under the age of fifteen, the highest percentage of younger people in southern Africa. With a population growing at the rate of 1.5 percent, Namibians will number about 2.6 million by 2025. A population density of about 6.5 people per square mile (2.5 per sq. km) makes Namibia one of the world's least densely populated nations. More than 90 percent of the country remains natural habitat. The high plains that run through the center of the country have most of the cities, townships, and farms. The Kalahari and Namib deserts support a very sparse population. Many parts of the waterless deserts along the Atlantic Ocean coast have no settlements.

◉ Ethnic Groups

Namibia's population—in ethnic terms—includes 87.5 percent black, 6 percent white, and 6.5 percent mixed-race citizens. Of Namibia's

black population, the Ovambo comprise about 50 percent of the total and make up the largest ethnic group in Namibia. Their homeland lies in the north, where Ovambo towns straddle the border with Angola. Higher rainfall in this region allows Ovambo farmers to raise crops and to graze large cattle herds. Some Ovambo have moved south to the cities or to work on commercial farms. The Ovambo played a prominent role in the fight for independence and make up the majority of political leaders and civil servants in Namibia.

Within Namibia the Ovambo are divided into eight subgroups: the Kwanyama (the largest), the Ndongo, the Kwambi, the Ngandjera, the Mbalantu, the Kwaluudhi, the Nkolokadhi, and the Eunda. A council and a chief govern each subgroup. Among the Ovambo, land is not privately owned. Instead, the chief allocates land to members of the group. Families live within fenced enclosures known as *eumbo*. A sacred fire is kept burning within the eumbo, from a log of mopane, the slow-burning wood of a local tree.

Members of the Ovambo work a field in northern Namibia.

The Kavango represent about 9 percent of the Namibian people. Their name comes from the Okavango River. The fertile land along this waterway provides rich soil and abundant fishing. During the civil war in Angola, which began in the 1970s, many Kavango fled into Namibia, doubling their population south of the border. As with the Ovambo, many are migrating south in search of work.

The Herero (about 7 percent of the population) took part in a historic uprising against colonists in the early twentieth century. They were defeated, with about half their numbers either killed or fleeing into the remote Kalahari Desert. A Bantu-speaking people, they traditionally raise cattle. A smaller group known as the Himba split away

THE HOLY FIRE

The Herero spend many of their evenings gathered around the *okuruo*, or holy fire. A Herero chief will gather members of the group. Seeking advice or the answer to a question, he speaks to the spirits of ancestors through the fire. The holy fire is also the place to confess mistakes and make promises to right any wrongs that have occurred. The Herero believe the fire must never go out.

from the Herero and moved into the Kaokoland, which lies along the Angola border. They too raise cattle. The Himba lead a difficult existence on sparse and arid land in their original place of settlement.

The Damara—making up about 7 percent of Namibians—are centered in Damaraland in the southern part of Kunene Province. Once desert hunters, they work as farmers, laborers, and miners. In the past, they were rivals of the Herero. Damara leaders allied with the Germans in the early twentieth century. The colonists set aside Damaraland for their use, but only about one-quarter of the Damara population still lives in this area.

The Nama are Khoisan speakers who live in southern Namibia and make up about 5 percent of the population. Many make their living as ranchers and livestock herders. Others are craft workers who create leatherwork, flutes, jewelry, and pottery.

The Caprivian population, including the Lozi, comprise about 4 percent of Namibians. They live at the eastern end of the Caprivi Strip, between the Chobe and Zambezi rivers. This fertile and well-watered area allows them to fish the local waterways and to raise livestock and crops.

The San make up about 3 percent of the population. Historians have estimated that they have been living in southern Africa as a distinct group for twenty-five thousand years. Many lived in the Kalahari Desert, and until the 1990s, some still led a hunter-gatherer lifestyle. This way of life has largely died out, however. As their hunting range was settled by farmers and ranchers, some San turned to trading and mining, while others became farmers or labored as hired hands on farms.

The Tswana are the smallest major ethnic group in Namibia, with about 0.5 percent of the population. Speaking a Bantu language, the Tswana people also live across the border in South Africa and in Botswana, a nation that was named for them.

HIMBA BEAUTY SECRETS

The women of the Himba tribe take care of their skin with a lotion made of ocher, butter, and a resin made from omuzumba, a kind of desert shrub. The lotion makes their skin a deep red color.

Namibians descended from European settlers represent about 6 percent of the population. Many trace their roots to German colonists who settled in Lüderitz and the surrounding area beginning in 1884. Others have Dutch ancestors from South Africa, who came north across the Orange River after World War I. People of European descent live mainly in central and southern Namibia, largely in cities and on commercial farms.

About 6.5 percent of all Namibians are of mixed African and European ancestry. They speak Afrikaans (the language of Dutch South Africa) or English and sometimes both. Most live in cities, including Windhoek, Keetmanshoop, Lüderitz, and Walvis Bay. The Basters, which make up about 2 percent of the total population, are included in this group. The Basters are the descendants of Dutch South Africans and black African peoples who moved north in the late 1860s and settled the town of Rehoboth. They founded a government under a *kaptein*, or chief, and a Volksraad, or council. They generally allied with the German settlers during the conflicts of the early twentieth century.

Women's Lives

Traditional cultural norms in Namibia place women in the role of housewife and mother. Many Namibians frown on women working

These women are pounding grain for the next meal. Most women in Namibia still work at home, but opportunities outside the home are becoming more available.

outside the home. Women hold few high government posts or seats in the legislature. Violence against women and children in the home has been an ongoing problem.

Some laws have been passed to improve women's legal rights. For example, the 1992 Labor Act set down the principle of equal pay for equal work. Other laws have improved women's rights to own land. With the permission of local councils, women can inherit communal land from their husbands. They can also keep the land if they remarry. The Traditional Authorities Act of 2000 requires gender balance in tribal governments. Women can join ruling councils and become chiefs, a role they never held while Namibia was a colony.

Languages

Although the official language of Namibia is English, fewer than 10 percent of the country's people speak it. By making English the official language, the Namibian government was seeking to avoid conflict over this decision among the country's different language groups. Namibia also sees the use of English as a way to put the country closer to the mainstream of the modern world economy, where English is the working language.

Nearly all Namibians speak at least two languages. Most ethnic groups have their own local dialects, often called a mother tongue. Many Namibians use Afrikaans to talk to one another. Afrikaans is a language related to Dutch. It was developed in South Africa when that nation was a Dutch colony. It is the first language of about 10 percent of the population—mostly blacks and mixed races, including Basters.

The German language arrived with German colonists in the late nineteenth century. German was the language of government and education before Namibia gained its independence. It remains the mother tongue of most of the European-descended inhabitants of Namibia. German newspapers circulate widely, while radio and television programs are commonly broadcast in the German language.

The two main African language families used in Namibia are Bantu and Khoisan. There are several hundred Bantu languages. These are spoken throughout sub-Saharan Africa (the region south

Learn a few simple phrases in two of Namibia's major languages.

English	Afrikaans	Ovambo
good morning	goeiemore	wa lalapo
good evening	goeienaand	wa tokelwapo
please	asseblief	ombili
thank you	dankie	tangi
excuse me	ekskuus	ombili manga

of the Sahara). Bantu speakers include the Ovambo and the Himba, while the San and other groups of southern Namibia speak Khoisan languages. Khoisan tongues are known for their use of sharp clicking noises, made by striking the tongue against different parts of the mouth and teeth. The San use four distinct clicks, for example. This feature makes Khoisan dialects difficult for outsiders to master.

Education

Before independence, Namibia had a limited system of public education. Many regions had no schools, and literacy among some groups was low. People who made their living at ranching or as farm laborers had little need for formal schooling. Traditional societies had their own way of training the young to survive by hunting and collecting water and food from the desert.

After independence in 1990, Namibia was unable to prepare young people for the modern global economy because of a shortage of teachers, schools, books, and shop facilities. A school construction program began in the 1990s. The new constitution makes education mandatory. Basic reading and writing classes have begun to improve literacy among adults. By the early twenty-first century, the literacy rate among the adult population had reached 80 percent.

Schooling among Namibians is compulsory between the ages of six and sixteen. Schools offer seven grades of primary education, followed by five years of secondary school. About 82 percent of primary school-age children attend school, while 38 percent of secondary-age children attend school. A legacy of the colonial era is private schools. Some conduct their classes in German. The official language of the country, English, is the language of instruction elsewhere. In some primary classes, Afrikaans or local Bantu languages are also used.

The University of Namibia in Windhoek offers higher education. The university opened in 1993. It offers courses in economics, education, medicine, and more. The Polytechnic of Namibia in Windhoek is a technical school with courses in engineering, business, and occupational courses in nursing, tourism, and hotel management.

A teacher helps students at a **primary school** in Rehoboth.

The **University of Namibia's main campus** is in Windhoek. The campus has more than seven thousand students.

Health

Namibia has many of the health problems affecting other nations in sub-Saharan Africa. Health care in the cities is generally good. But many Namibians in rural areas or in the townships on the outskirts of the cities have little access to doctors or clinics.

Yet the country has achieved a rate of life expectancy—52 years—that is the highest in southern Africa. (It is low, however, compared to world standards, where life expectancies often extend into the 70s.) Men live 50 years on average, while women average 53 years. The rate of infant mortality, or the number of babies who die within a year of their birth, stands at 55 per 1,000 births. This is a relatively low rate in sub-Saharan Africa, although quite high by world standards.

One of the most serious health problems, in Namibia and throughout Africa, is human immunodeficiency virus (HIV). The rate of HIV infection has been rising, and more than two hundred thousand

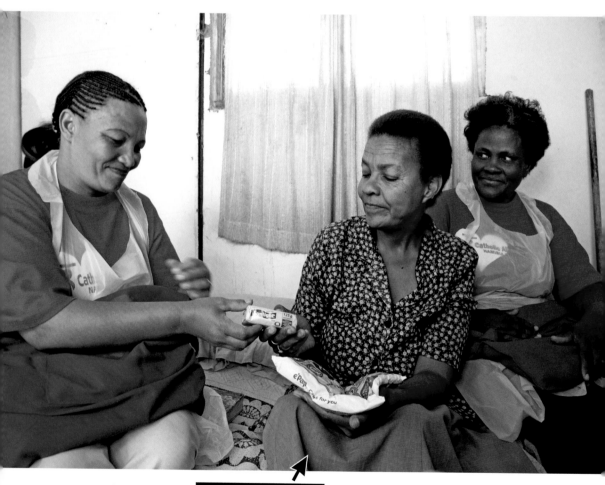

Volunteers visit a woman living with HIV (center). Nearly 60 percent of the people living with HIV and AIDS in Namibia are women.

Namibians carry the virus. HIV is spread through sexual contact or through contaminated blood. The disease can lead to AIDS. Many AIDS patients in Namibia have limited access to treatment or medicine. About 21 percent of the adult population carries the HIV virus, among the highest rates in the world.

Other common health problems in Namibia include pneumonia and tuberculosis. Malaria, which is spread by the bite of a mosquito, is a big problem in the northern provinces. The country is fighting malaria by donating bed nets to families. The nets protect people from the insects at night. Some pilot projects for spraying mosquito-breeding areas have been undertaken in Namibia's rivers and wetlands.

For up-to-date health care news from Namibia, visit www.vgsbooks.com for links. Learn more about what travelers should do to prepare for a visit to Namibia.

CULTURAL LIFE

Namibia's modern society and culture have complex roots that extend thousands of years into the past. First settled by Khoisan-speaking hunter-gatherers, the region experienced a wave of Bantu migration that caused ongoing conflict over land and resources. The divide between hunters and settled farmers endured through the time of settlement by Europeans and their descendants. To this day, Namibians identify themselves with a particular ethnic group and clan first and as members of the Namibian nation second. This diversity and complexity add to the nation's rich and varied culture.

◉ Religion

Christianity is the main religion in Namibia, with about 90 percent of the population belonging to a Christian church. Missionaries who arrived from Europe in the late nineteenth century brought this faith to what was then German Southwest Africa. Lutheranism is an important Christian sect in Germany. At least half of all Christians

in Namibia are members of the Lutheran Church. Christian doctrine has resulted in a decline in many traditional practices in Namibia such as polygyny, or the marriage of one man to two or more wives.

Traditional beliefs have survived among African ethnic groups, especially in rural areas. About 10 percent of Namibia's people follow various traditional beliefs. It is common among the San people, for example, to believe in the spirits of their ancestors. They believe that these spirits remain active and play an important role in their fortunes. Religious diviners have a variety of methods for foretelling the future, and spiritual healers call on ancestors and spirits of the sky and earth to assist in curing illness.

In the past, the Herero held elaborate religious ceremonies at important life events, such as births, weddings, funerals, and the passage into adulthood. Cattle were an essential part of Herero life and were held to be sacred animals, manifesting ancestral spirits.

The majority of Namibians are Christian. This **Lutheran church** was built in the early part of the twentieth century in the center of Windhoek.

In modern times, this aspect of Herero life has been largely lost, and traditional religious ceremonies are becoming rare.

Folktales and Literature

Namibians have been telling stories since the distant past. Nama storytellers relate traditional folktales known as *izes*. Many of these stories describe animals that take on human form and cause mischief among ordinary people. The San and Damara enjoy stories about magic and supernatural events.

Some folktales have been adapted from European stories brought by colonists. The best-known modern writers of Namibia have European and African roots. Books of the early twentieth century describe the complex experience of people living within a colony divided among several ethnic groups. Gustav Frenssen wrote *Peter Moor's Journey to Southwest Africa* in 1905. Henno Martin's *The Sheltering Desert* of 1956 was written from the author's experience as a geologist on the run from the colonial authorities during World War II.

One of Namibia's best-known contemporary novelists is Joseph Diescho, who wrote the autobiographical *Born of the Sun* in 1988. In this book, Diescho describes his life as a mine laborer and his fight for Namibian independence. Diescho followed this work with *Troubled Waters* in 1993.

Giselher Hoffmann, a writer of German descent, deals with Namibian history and modern events. *Im Bunde der Dritte* (In the Third Band) explores the subject of poaching, while *Die Erstgeboren* (The Firstborn) describes conflict between San and German settlers. Richard Kunzmann, who was born in Namibia, writes crime fiction set in South Africa.

Media

Namibia has four major daily newspapers. Its best-selling newspaper is the *Namibian*, founded by Gwen Lister in 1986. The paper took a proindependence point of view. Printed in English and Ovambo, it was the target of several attacks during the struggle for independence. Recently the *Namibian* has emerged as an important voice against government corruption.

The government of Namibia, which suppresses antigovernment writing, publishes the *Namibian News*. *Die Republikein* (the Republic) was started in 1977 and has articles and columns in English, Afrikaans, and German. A German daily, the *Allgemeine Zeitung* (General Newspaper), also appears in Windhoek to serve the country's large German-speaking community. First appearing in 1916, this paper is Namibia's oldest. Monthly magazines include *Namibia Review* and *Abacus*, both published in English.

The Namibian Broadcasting Corporation operates a nationwide television service as well as a radio station. One Africa Television

Two men run an issue of the *Namibian,* the major newspaper in Windhoek.

broadcasts information and entertainment, with some programming from the United States and Europe. The government is wary of foreign programming, however, and bars shows that appear to criticize the administration. Some shows have been banned entirely from the airwaves. Many Namibians lack television sets. They turn to radio for information. Kanaal 7 is a radio station broadcast in Afrikaans and English, with a Christian religious theme.

Namibia also has developed a small film industry. The country's rugged landscapes make it a favored shooting location for South African producers.

◉ Crafts

Skilled artisans in Namibia create a wide variety of craft and household objects made from local resources. Many sell their wares through local cooperatives, found on the main streets of towns throughout the country.

Using dyed strips taken from the Makalani palm, the Ovambo and Herero peoples make baskets in many shapes. The Herero also fashion elaborate dolls dressed in nineteenth-century costumes, a style that Herero women adopted from European missionaries.

Other groups have their own specialties. The Basters, who live around Rehoboth, are skilled weavers well known for karosses, or blankets, as well as rugs and tapestries. The San people make necklaces and amulets (pendants) from beads and ostrich shell, as well as leather sandals, iron arrows, and toys. Their beadwork decorates accessories such as shoes, hats, and handbags. The Himba are famous for a head ornament known as the *oruvanda*, worn by women and made from iron beads and leather.

Leatherworkers use the hides of cattle, sheep, and game for leather. The hides are tinted with plant dyes

ELEPHANT PAPER

Namibian companies have created some new ways to make paper. The Onankali Omahangu Paper Project was set up in 2002. The group makes paper from pearl millet, a staple grain grown throughout Africa. The millet is cut and the leaves of the plant are mixed with recycled paper. The stuff is mashed, dyed, and rolled into sheets.

Another company, Magical Elephant Creations, uses something else—elephant dung. Because elephants don't digest rough vegetation very well, their droppings are fibrous and make good paper. The dung is high in cellulose and doesn't smell bad. From this very raw material, Magical Elephant Creations makes paper, envelopes, diaries, and cards.

and ocher. The leather goes into pouches and bags, clothing, sandals, shoes, belts, and handbags. Caprivians of the northeast make wooden masks, drums, pottery, leather goods, and stone carvings. The Damara as well as the Ovambo are known for woodworking. Using hand tools, they shape weapons, tools, masks, furniture, musical instruments, toys, and walking sticks.

Music

European and African musical traditions mix in Namibia, where people have taken up musical trends popular throughout the African continent, including hip-hop, reggae, and highlife. Traditional tribal music has also brought some interesting musical trends. The *shumbo* is a popular style that originated with the Ovambo. It combines modern instruments such as the guitar with traditional drums and handheld percussion instruments. *Kwaito* music comes from South Africa. It has adopted hip-hop, reggae, rhythm and blues, and other recent popular styles. Kwaito singers create their own rhymes and verses to a recorded track, which plays as an accompaniment.

The San play a great variety of instruments, including musical bows, guitars, and lamellophones (small instruments with reeds or tines that are plucked with the fingers). The *seganpure* is a type of violin made of a long, thin stick and a single string, which is tuned with a peg at one end. Some believe that the San created the seganpure after they saw European violins.

Bantu-speaking peoples, such as the Herero and the Himba, have their own music. Singers perform songs of praise as groups of workers chant complex harmonies while laboring in fields, leading cattle to pasture, or milking cows. Work songs are also popular among the Ovambo, who have a wealth of traditional stories set to music. The

THE TROUBLE WITH SHEBEENS

A favorite place in Namibia for music and fun is a shebeen. These are informal dance clubs set up in an empty building, such as a store or a house. Some people build their shebeens with wooden beams, plywood walls, and a roof made of iron sheets. Many poor and unemployed women in townships set up shebeens to make a living.

The government frowns on shebeens, however. It claims that they often attract noisy and unruly crowds and are a threat to public order. A new law recently banned them. In response, shebeen owners throughout the country protested. They formed the Namibian Shebeen Association to fight the law. The outcome of the controversy is still uncertain.

Ovambo favor European choir music, especially multipart religious and patriotic songs. The Nama have also adopted choir singing, brought by missionaries in the nineteenth century.

Rock and roll arrived in Namibia in the late twentieth century. Die Vogel is a German band that gained a wide following in Windhoek during the 1970s. Other popular performers are Ngatu, a guitarist, and Ras Sheehama, who has performed in Europe and the Caribbean. Sunny Boy, another singer, combined hip-hop and kwaito music into a brand-new genre he dubbed HiKwa.

Namibian ethnic groups have a set of dances that are performed at social gatherings and important events such as weddings. For example, the Nama Step is a dance to the accompaniment of guitars and accordion, sometimes with drums and flutes added.

▷ Sports

Namibians are united by a passion for football (also known as soccer) and the fortunes of the national football team, the Brave Warriors. The team qualified for the African Cup in 1998 but was eliminated from competition in the first round. International matches take place in the Independence Stadium in Windhoek.

Other sports popular in Namibia include cricket and rugby, which arrived with British South African settlers in 1916. Namibia has produced many skilled rugby players, many of whom play for professional squads in South Africa. The national rugby team is called the Welwitschias. The team qualified for the World Cup, the international rugby championship, in 1999, 2003, and 2007. Namibians also take a strong interest in track and field. Sprinter Frankie Fredericks inspired

A **Namibian rugby player** *(left)* **goes after the ball during a 2007 World Cup match against Georgia.**

the entire country with his Olympic silver medals in 1992 and 1996.

The deserts and mountains of Namibia challenge hikers and mountain climbers. On the coast, the cold waters of the Benguela Current attract surfers, divers, and windsurfers.

Clothing

European dress is common in Namibian cities and towns. Hats are common gear to protect against the sun, and light and loose clothing keeps people cool in hot weather. Namibians dress more formally than many other African peoples and Europeans. They may frown on outsiders who arrive in too-casual dress. Suits and ties are still required clothing for men in many white-collar occupations. Many churches and museums have strict dress codes.

Clothing adapted to the climate is still the norm in many parts of the country. Himba men of the northwest, for example, still wear small leather thongs or loincloths, while women wear short skirts made of leather. Himba women also favor leather bands around the neck, a garment that makes them appear tall and their bodies longer.

German missionaries who arrived in southern Namibia in the nineteenth century found that Herero women wore very little in the hot climate. They had them dress up in a fashion that was popular in Europe: dresses with long sleeves, frilly fronts, and petticoats reaching to the ground. This tradition lives on, although such outfits are largely ceremonial.

Food

The hearty cuisine of Namibia draws from the cooking traditions of the country's ethnic groups, alongside menus imported from South Africa and Europe (particularly Germany). The country's cattle-raising tradition has made it a nation of avid meat eaters, who favor beef and mutton (sheep) as well as game meat such as zebra, ostrich, and crocodile. One favorite method of preparing meat is to cut it into strips, season

The Namibian rugby team is named after a truly weird plant, the welwitschia. It survives only in the arid wasteland of the Namib Desert. This plant grows a sturdy central trunk and a pair of floppy green leaves. The leaves creep sideways and continue to enlarge throughout the plant's life—which can last more than one thousand years. The leaves are constantly ripped by the desert winds, giving the appearance of a massive, braided tangle of vegetation. The biggest welwitschias grow to 4 feet (1.2 m) high and 12 feet (3.7 m) in diameter.

it, add vinegar as a preservative, and then dry it—a preparation known throughout southern Africa as biltong. Near the coast, a variety of seafood is served, including lobster, steenbras, kingklip, and kabeljou.

The Namibian *braai* is an outdoor cookout over a grill (often a pit in the ground) fired by wood charcoal. The braai, which originated in South Africa, is a popular social occasion all over Namibia. Cooks prepare a stew known as *potije*, made by mixing tomatoes, onions, cabbage, pumpkins, and other vegetables and meat (beef, goat, mutton, or fish) in a three-legged iron pot.

Other popular dishes include mealie soup, a thin soup made from cornmeal. The Ovambo people use millet in soups, stews, and *oshikundu*, an alcoholic drink. The San have subsisted for centuries on food found in the desert: small game, lizards, ostrich eggs, and edible cacti. German colonists brought a taste for sausage, beer, and the sweet pastry dessert known as strudel. *Landjager* is a sausage made from beef and pork that makes a snack for all occasions.

Squash in many forms—pumpkins and butternut, for example—is cooked in stews and served fried or baked. Fruits, mostly imported from other regions in Africa, include kiwi, bananas, oranges, avocados, and pineapples.

OSHIFIMA

Oshifima is a thick cornmeal porridge popular in Namibia. Namibians often hollow out a center within a ball of porridge and place the meal's main course inside.

1 cup water

1 cup milk

¾ plus ½ cups white cornmeal

1. Boil water in a small saucepan. Pour milk into a medium bowl, and slowly add ¾ cup of cornmeal, stirring constantly until you have a thick paste.
2. Carefully pour the cornmeal paste into the boiling water and stir. Continue to stir over heat for 4 to 5 minutes.
3. Add ½ cup cornmeal, and stir until the porridge thickens. It will pull away from the side of the pan when ready.
4. Scrape the porridge into a lightly greased serving bowl and let cool.
5. Use your hands to form the porridge into a ball. Place it in the center of the bowl and serve.

Serves 4

Visit www.vgsbooks.com for links to websites with more traditional Namibian recipes.

Holidays

Namibia has a full calendar of civic and religious holidays. The most solemn civic holiday is Independence Day on March 21, which marks Namibia's achievement of self-rule in 1990. Workers Day takes place on May 1. Cassinga Day is on May 4. On this day, Namibians commemorate a battle that took place in 1978, when South African paratroopers attacked a SWAPO base in the town of Cassinga, Angola. The battle resulted in the deaths of civilian refugees as well as SWAPO members and shifted world opinion in favor of Namibian independence.

Maharero Day, also known as Heroes Day, occurs on a weekend in late August. A parade and celebration in Okahandja celebrates the deeds of Herero freedom fighters in wars against the German colonists in the early twentieth century. Herero women often walk in the parades dressed in their long, nineteenth-century dresses. Africa Day on May 25 marks the establishment of the Organization of African Unity, a group set up in 1963 to promote the unity of African nations. Human Rights Day falls on December 10. This occasion was inspired by a conflict that took place in 1959 in a township near Windhoek, when several thousand black Namibians resisted forced removal.

Namibian Christians observe traditional religious holidays such as Christmas and Easter. Good Friday, Easter Monday, and Ascension Day (on May 17) are national holidays, when most public and private offices are closed. Family Day, a Christmas season celebration, takes place on December 26. Some traditional African groups hold lengthy ceremonies at important events such as weddings and funerals. These solemn observances sometimes involve a holiday from ordinary work and travel for several days.

THE ECONOMY

After independence Namibia opened the country to outside investment and built new manufacturing and service industries. Laws ban the government from seizing private companies and also allow foreign firms to control their earnings and investment capital. Namibia has also taken a practical approach to land reform. It has passed laws that prevent the government from seizing agricultural land without compensation to the owner.

The Namibian dollar has a one-to-one conversion with the rand, the currency of South Africa. This conversion links Namibia closely with the much larger economy of its southern neighbor. South Africa remains an important trading partner and a source of foreign investment.

Namibia earns income from manufacturing, agriculture, mining, and tourism. The country has abundant natural resources—particularly useful minerals, precious gemstones, and fertile agricultural land. It is one of the most productive national economies in Africa, with a high per capita income in relation to its neighbors.

In the first years of the twenty-first century, the gross domestic product (GDP)—the total of all goods and services produced within the country—was growing at the rate of about 4 percent every year. This figure was about average for the countries in southern Africa. In 2004 the Namibian GDP reached $4.8 billion, or about $2,370 per person. This is a low figure compared to South Africa but is average among Namibia's other neighboring countries. New transportation projects, such as the Trans-Caprivi Highway and a bridge across the Zambezi River to link Namibia and Zambia, have improved Namibia's links with neighboring countries. Namibia has also improved the port of Walvis Bay, making it one of the busiest commercial harbors on Africa's Atlantic coastline.

Per capita income in 2005 reached almost $7,500, a high figure among southern African countries. However, wealth is not spread evenly. A small segment of the population controls most private business and earns a large share of the income. About half of the people

TROPHY TOURISM

Trophy hunting is an important part of the Namibian economy. Many wealthy tourists come to hunt wild game *(below)*. They hire guides to lead them through the bush in search of antelope and other game. The animals are sometimes first bought at auction or from livestock ranches. They are then released to roam reserves where hunters purchase licenses to track and kill the animals.

live in poverty. Namibian cities also have a high unemployment rate. In the countryside, many families live as subsistence farmers, growing only enough food to survive. Many of these people have no land of their own and little hope of a brighter future.

◉ Services and Tourism

Services provide about 58 percent of the GDP in Namibia, making this the largest sector of the economy. Service businesses, which employ about 33 percent of the labor force, include insurance, retail stores, marketing, banking, tourism, and government jobs such as teaching. As the country draws more foreign investment and as more Namibians reach the middle class, income rises and the demand for services increases.

Tourism has become a major sector of the Namibian economy. Visitors arrive from Europe and South Africa to see the nation's wildlife and to explore its stark deserts, coastal regions, and national parks. Namibia devotes much of its income from tourism to conservation of its wildlife and natural habitat.

The country is especially favored by travelers from Germany, the

nation that colonized Namibia in the late nineteenth century. Many Namibian towns reveal this heritage through traditional German architecture, cuisine, and culture.

Manufacturing, Mining, and Energy

Industry and mining make up 30 percent of the economy and employ about 20 percent of the labor force. Mining represents Namibia's largest export sector. Namibian mines produce more nonfuel minerals (such as diamonds, copper, and lead) than any other country in Africa. The country is also an important producer of uranium (an element used in nuclear reactors).

Diamond mining represents more than 80 percent of all mining income. Diamond mining is extensive in Oranjemund and in the countryside near Lüderitz. The stones are created naturally under immense pressure deep within the ground. Movements in the earth's crust sometimes thrust them to the surface. They are then washed down rivers and streams and collect just beneath the surface. These deposits are mined on private reserves, where Namibia produces more than one million carats of diamonds each year—about 5 percent of global output. Namibia's first diamond-cutting factory was built in 2003 in Windhoek.

Namibian mines also produce copper, uranium, lead, gold, salt, sulfur, silver, tin, and zinc. In recent years, as mining companies have removed all the available ores from underground deposits, several mines have closed. The companies have been forced to explore for new sources of ore in more remote areas, where digging and processing the ore is more difficult. New exploration and prospecting, however,

THE KARAKUL ARRIVE AND THRIVE

The international trade in Karakul sheep began in 1902 with a German merchant named Paul Thorer. He sent sixty-nine sheep from Uzbekistan, a desert nation in central Asia, to Germany. The sheep did not adapt well to the cold, damp climate of Europe, so twelve were sent on to German Southwest Africa. At a large ranch near Windhoek, the Karakul sheep thrived in the dry climate. Namibian breeders developed a unique kind of white Karakul pelt (skin), known as Swakara, for South-West African Karakul.

As furs went out of style, people around the world also lost their interest in Karakul pelts. Namibian sheep raisers adapted by breeding the sheep for carpet wool, which is taken from living adult sheep. Since then the market for Karakul carpets has thrived.

This equipment is used to clean **uranium** ore. Namibia is one of the top ten uranium-producing countries in the world.

depend on a high market price for mineral resources. This high price makes investment worthwhile for Namibian and foreign companies.

Namibia has explored for natural gas as well as oil with limited success. The Kudu Field, a large field of natural gas, lies offshore near the mouth of the Orange River. Extracting the gas requires specialized equipment and skilled crews. Several companies have proposed investment and operations in the field to develop these reserves. They would produce an energy fuel that is less polluting than products made from crude oil.

Manufacturing has been a limited part of the economy of Namibia. Namibian industry has had to compete with South Africa, a larger and more industrialized nation. In addition, Namibia's pool of laborers for manufacturing is small. As a result, the country imports many finished products, such as automobiles and computers. Namibia also imports most heavy machinery and consumer products, mostly from South Africa.

Within the industry sector, manufacturing makes up about 13 percent of the GDP. It employs 5 percent of the labor force. Textile factories in Windhoek make finished cloth, while food-processing factories make beer, soft drinks, and canned foods.

Agriculture and Fishing

Farming and herding provide about 12 percent of GDP and employ about 47 percent of the labor force. This includes subsistence farmers. The most important crops are millet, sorghum, and corn. Some farmers in southwestern Namibia raise vegetables and fruit in the Orange River valley. Northern Namibia also supports some crop farming.

Namibian ranchers are the most significant sector of the farming economy. They raise livestock for meat and hides. Cattle ranches are common in the plains of central and northern Namibia. Ranchers in the drier south raise sheep, goats, and ostriches.

Because of the history of uneven distribution of land in Namibia, the agriculture sector is sharply divided. Subsistence farmers, most of whom are black Africans, struggle to raise crops on small plots of land. Commercial farms, on the other hand, are typically owned by white Namibians and take up a large percentage of the country's rich pasture and crop lands. These farms earn a lot of money by exporting the livestock and crops they raise. The Namibian government has tried to more fairly divide landownership through redistribution programs. These programs pay owners to make some of their land available for sale.

THE EPUPA DAM CONTROVERSY

The government of Namibia is planning to build a large hydroelectric dam on the Kunene River, in the northwest along the border with Angola. The dam would be 600 feet (183 m) high, making it the tallest dam in Africa. It would create a huge reservoir and generate power to create enough electricity for the entire country.

But the Himba people are not happy about the Epupa Dam. The water that would back up behind the dam would destroy fertile land and pasture for their livestock. In addition, much of the local wildlife would disappear. The large reservoir would make it hard to travel from one side of the river to the other. The small army of construction workers would have to be housed in temporary work towns, disrupting local society and bringing a risk of overcrowding and crime.

The government insists the dam will be built, however. It sees the dam creating new jobs and benefiting the entire country by providing a clean source of energy.

Rich fishing grounds exist in the waters off the Namibian coast. The Benguela Current provides nutrients for a variety of fish and shellfish. In the past, foreign fleets overfished these waters. Before independence, Namibia was unable to enforce strict limits on fishing its coastal waters. By the 1980s, fish were becoming increasingly scarce, and the annual catches were dwindling. In 1990, the year of independence, Namibia declared a 200-mile (322 km) offshore boundary. Within this limit, only Namibian boats can fish commercially. The new extended fishing zone has greatly improved the nation's fishing business.

Namibia takes in about 60,000 tons (54,431 metric tons) of fish every year, making its fishing industry as big as that of Canada or Norway. Commercial fish include anchovies, hake, mackerel, and sardines. Deep waters contain schools of tuna and sole, as well as crabs and lobsters. Fish canneries on the Atlantic coast employ workers in Walvis Bay and Lüderitz.

These men work at a **fish factory** in Walvis Bay. They are packing hake for shipment to Europe.

Trade

Exports are a vital source of income to the Namibian economy. The country's most important trading partner, South Africa, is the source of most imported goods and the market for the majority of exports. Namibia also exports to the United Kingdom and the nations of Western Europe, which buy an increasing amount of Namibian meat and fish. The most important exports include diamonds, fish, grapes, and beef. Namibia also has a growing export business in clothing to the United States. The country imports heavy equipment, especially for manufacturing and mining. It also imports oil, transportation equipment, chemicals, and industrial machinery.

Increased trade with China has been a big development in recent years. China has invested in Namibian mineral resources and has extended grants and interest-free loans to the country. Trade with China is controversial, however, as inexpensive Chinese textiles and other goods are making Namibian industries uncompetitive.

Namibia belongs to the Southern African Customs Union (SACU) with South Africa, Botswana, Lesotho, and Swaziland. There are no tariffs (taxes on imports) on goods moving among these nations. The SACU, with headquarters in Windhoek, is seeking a free-trade agreement with the United States. If successful, this agreement would ease trade with the world's leading economy and boost the economy of Namibia.

Transportation and Communication

Namibia benefits from a well-developed road system. Of the 26,245 miles (42,237 km) of Namibian roads, 3,359 miles (5,406 km) are paved. Major cities are linked by road to the country's borders and to ports along the coast. The Trans-Caprivi Highway runs through the Caprivi region, linking Namibia to its neighbors to the east. Another major road under construction, the Trans-Kalahari, will improve traffic between southeastern Africa and the port of Walvis Bay.

The deepwater port of Walvis Bay is one of the busiest harbors on the Atlantic coast of Africa. A large container port there handles shipping for Namibia's landlocked neighbors, Zambia and Botswana. Walvis Bay has also become the center of the Namibian fishing industry.

The main Namibian railway runs from the border with South Africa to Windhoek and Walvis Bay. Branch lines run north to Grootfontein and to Lüderitz. Transnamib Starline Passenger Services, the rail company, links Windhoek with the town of Upington in South Africa.

Namibia's main airport is Chief Hosea Kutako International Airport, just east of Windhoek. Several airlines link Namibia directly with the United Kingdom and Germany. Other international travelers

This road, the **B1 highway,** runs from the Angolan border, curves south through Windhoek, and continues to the border with South Africa.

must fly first to South Africa and take a second flight between that country and Windhoek.

Namibia has a good phone system, with almost 150,000 fixed lines and about half a million cell phones. As in many regions of Africa, cell phones serve a majority of the population and are favored over less reliable (and often more expensive) landlines. Some farming settlements and small villages lack phone service entirely. The Internet has reached about seventy-five thousand households, most in Windhoek and other major towns. Internet cafés are a convenient and cheap way for people to browse the World Wide Web, check e-mail, and chat with friends. About thirty-five hundred Internet hosts allow Namibian subscribers access to the system.

Visit www.vgsbooks.com for links to websites with more information about Namibia's economy.

The Future

Namibia benefits from a wealth of valuable natural resources as well as political stability. The country has avoided civil strife and has achieved independence relatively peacefully. Social and ethnic divisions still occur, and the economic benefits of a modern economy have not reached all segments of the population. Nevertheless, most Namibians feel they have some representation in the legislature. In addition, they have the freedom to safely express their views.

The most serious threats to Namibia's future are related to the environment and public health. The AIDS epidemic that has ravaged Africa and particularly southern Africa has not spared Namibia. A growing population of AIDS orphans has been created, and the strain of caring for AIDS patients severely tests the public health system. The country's natural habitat is under pressure from the growth of cities and a burgeoning tourism industry. Water resources are limited and are sparking conflict with Namibia's neighbors over the use of shared waterways. A long drought has affected agriculture as well.

The country has attracted foreign investment, which is crucial for manufacturing industries, technology companies, and mining. Increased trade with China—the world's most populous nation—also promises to be a major factor in the success of the future Namibian economy. Although Namibia is distant from the world's main trade routes, it does offer a welcoming climate to businesses and to individuals, who arrive as tourists and as new residents. Tying the Namibian currency to the South African rand means that Namibia also benefits from economic growth in its much larger and wealthier neighbor to the south. With an open economy and calm among the different political factions and ethnic groups, Namibians can look forward to a prosperous future.

AREA 318,696 square miles (825,418 sq. km)

MAIN LANDFORMS Brandberg Mountains, Huns Mountains, Bushveld, Central Plateau, Escarpment, Etosha Salt Pan, Kalahari Desert, Namib Desert

HIGHEST POINT Königstein, 8,550 feet (2,606 m)

LOWEST POINT Sea level

MAJOR RIVERS Kunene, Okavango, Orange, Zambezi, Chobe, Ekuma

ANIMALS African buffalo, antelopes, brown hyenas, cheetahs, elands, elephants, giraffes, impalas, jackals, lions, rhinoceroses, monitor lizards, Nile crocodiles, puff adders, spitting cobras, springbok, vervet monkeys, warthogs, wild dogs, wildebeests, zebras

CAPITAL CITY Windhoek

OTHER MAJOR CITIES Lüderitz, Walvis Bay

OFFICIAL LANGUAGE English

MONETARY UNIT Namibian dollar. 100 cents = 1 Namibian dollar.

CURRENCY

The official currency of Namibia is the Namibian dollar. The government issued this currency for the first time in 1993, replacing the South African rand. The Namibian dollar is divided into 100 cents. Banknotes are printed in denominations of 10, 20, 50, 100, and 200 dollars. Coins are minted in denominations of 5, 10, and 50 cents, and of 1 dollar and 5 dollars. Hendrik Witbooi, a chief of the Nama people, is shown on all Namibian banknotes. The rand is still legal tender in Namibia. It can be converted into Namibian dollars at par, meaning 1 rand is worth 1 Namibian dollar. About 7 Namibian dollars equal 1 U.S. dollar.

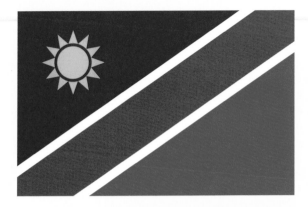

The flag of Namibia was officially adopted on March 21, 1990, the date of Namibia's independence from South Africa. It is based on the design of the flag of the South West Africa People's Organization. It consists of three diagonal bands: blue in the upper left; red in the middle of the flag, set off with narrow white borders; and green in the bottom right. In the upper left is a sun with twelve rays. The red stands for the people of Namibia, the blue for the country's water and natural resources, green for agriculture, and white for peace.

After winning independence, Namibia held a national competition for a new national anthem. A composer and musician named Axali Doeseb won the contest with *Namibia, Land of the Brave*. The anthem was performed for the first time on the first anniversary of independence, in 1991.

Namibia, Land of the Brave
Namibia land of the brave
Freedom fight we have won
Glory to their bravery
Whose blood waters our freedom
We give our love and loyalty
Together in unity
Contrasting beautiful Namibia
Namibia our country
Beloved land of savannahs
Hold high the banner of liberty

CHORUS
Namibia our Country
Namibia Motherland
We love thee

Famous People

LIBERTINA AMATHILA (b. 1940) A physician and politician born in Walvis Bay, Amathila became president of the World Health Organization, an agency of the UN, in 2000, when she was serving as Namibia's minister of health. She was active in working for AIDS patients in Namibia and became a prominent spokesperson for African nations on the issue of international aid to combat the disease. She was named deputy prime minister of Namibia in 2005.

JOSEPH DIESCHO (b. 1955) A novelist born in Andara, Diescho studied law at Fort Hare University in South Africa. He worked for a year in a diamond mine but then returned to his studies. The South African government briefly arrested and imprisoned him for speaking out against the apartheid system. He also attended university in Hamburg, Germany, and Columbia University in New York. His books, including *Born of the Sun* and *Troubled Waters*, describe the struggles of people caught up in the Namibian war of independence.

FRANKIE FREDERICKS (b. 1967) An Olympic track star born in Windhoek, Fredericks is the most famous athlete in Namibia. He attended Brigham Young University in the United States. At the World Track Championships in 1991, he won a silver medal in the 200-meter race. He won two more silver medals, in the 100- and 200-meter races, at the Summer Olympics in Barcelona, Spain, in 1992. He performed the same feat in the 1996 Olympics in Atlanta, Georgia. Fredericks was the first Namibian to win an Olympic medal.

ADOLPH JENTSCH (1888–1977) An artist born in Dresden, Germany, Jentsch moved to Namibia in 1938 as Germany prepared for war. He settled in a small town named Dordabis and painted pictures of the surrounding countryside. His watercolor and oil paintings are collector's items in Namibia.

JACKSON KAUJEUA (b. 1953) Kaujeua is a renowned musician and composer born in the small town of Huns. He trained at a music college in South Africa, but the nation's government forced him to leave the country for opposing the South African policy of apartheid. Kaujeua moved to Great Britain, where he formed the group Black Diamond, featuring traditional Namibian music. After Namibia won independence, he returned to his homeland.

GWEN LISTER (b. 1953) A journalist and newspaper publisher born in East London, South Africa, Lister studied at the University of Cape Town and then moved to Windhoek. In 1978 she started the *Windhoek Observer*. She left this newspaper and founded the *Namibian* in 1985. The name was an act of defiance, as the country was still ruled by South Africa and its official name was South-West Africa. Her strong stand against South African occupation of Namibia helped to rally people behind the movement for independence.

SAMUEL MAHARERO (1856–1923) A leader of the Herero fight against the German colonists, Maharero was born in Okahandja and became a chief of the Herero as a young man. He organized a revolt in 1904. A bounty was placed on Maharero's head, but he managed to elude the German reinforcements sent against him. His rebellion was crushed at the battle at Waterberg in August 1904. Then Maharero led a band of Herero into Botswana, where he died. His life is celebrated each year on Heroes Day, also known as Maharero Day, in Namibia.

MICHELLE MCLEAN (b. 1973) Born in Windhoek, McLean is a model who won the 1992 Miss Universe pageant, held in Bangkok, Thailand. In the same year, she founded a nonprofit group known as the Children's Trust, which helps poor children get care and schooling. She helped Namibia host the Miss Universe contest in 1995.

NGATUKONDJE NGANJONE (b. 1975) A musician born in Old Farm, Zambia, Nganjone traveled with his family as they were living as refugees from the conflict in Namibia. They finally returned to Namibia at independence in 1990. Nganjone formed a band while in high school and developed a new sound combining shumbo (an Ovambo style) with Afrobeat and reggae styles. He released a CD, *Biggest Gift*, which found a big audience in Namibia.

SAM NUJOMA (b. 1929) The first president of Namibia was born in Ongandjera in northern Namibia. He became the president of the South West Africa People's Organization (SWAPO) in 1960. He was reelected in 1994, winning about three-quarters of the popular vote and again in 1999 when the constitution was changed to allow him another term. He remains the head of SWAPO, the strongest political party in the country.

HERMAN ANDIMBA TOIVO JA TOIVO (b. 1924) Born in northern Namibia, Toivo founded the Ovamboland People's Congress in 1957. The organization would later become SWAPO. He led the struggle against South Africa and for Namibian independence. He became the SWAPO secretary-general but was arrested and imprisoned by South Africa in 1966 and held for eighteen years. After independence he became Namibia's minister of mines.

HENDRIK WITBOOI (1825–1905) Born in southwestern Namibia, Witbooi was a chief of the Nama. He fought against the rival Herero people and allied the Nama with the German troops in German Southwest Africa. In 1904 he led a revolt against German rule of the colony. He was killed in battle the next year, becoming a symbol of Namibia's drive for independence. Witbooi's portrait is printed on all modern Namibian banknotes.

ETOSHA NATIONAL PARK This wildlife refuge in northern Namibia is home to more than one hundred mammal species. The park surrounds a large, flat salt pan that turns into a lagoon during rains and hosts a great variety of thirsty mammals and birds.

FISH RIVER CANYON The Fish River has cut this deep gorge in the rugged highlands of southern Namibia. The canyon is 100 miles (160 km) long and in some places more than 1,640 feet (500 m) deep.

HOBA METEORITE The world's largest known meteorite landed about eighty thousand years ago in north central Namibia, near the present-day town of Grootfontein. It is made of iron, nickel, and cobalt and weighs about 119,050 pounds (54,000 kilograms).

KALAHARI DESERT The Kalahari straddles the eastern border of Namibia with Botswana. The Kalahari is the ancient home of the San, who have hunted on its dry plains for thousands of years.

KHAUDOM GAME RESERVE The Namibian government has set aside this large area of scrub and wildlife as a preserve, where hunting and large-scale development is banned. The reserve runs along the border with Botswana. Elephants, zebras, hyenas, and other large mammals roam freely among the dry salt pans and ridges of sand and rock.

NAMIB-NAUKLUFT NATIONAL PARK The large, shifting sand dunes of this region are constantly moved and shaped by the wind. The park, the size of Switzerland, is the largest game reserve on the African continent.

SKELETON COAST This barren desert in northern Namibia lies along the Atlantic Ocean. It was named for the bodies of sailors that came ashore and soon died in a waterless wasteland, leaving only their skeletons behind.

SOSSUSVLEI A vast sand sea, the Sossusvlei region lies in western Namibia. This area contains the highest and oldest sand dunes in the world, which shift constantly in the prevailing winds from the ocean to the west.

TWYFELFONTEIN More than two thousand ancient petroglyphs, or designs in rock, have survived at this site. These petroglyphs show many animals, including giraffes, rhinos, lions, elephants, and a sea lion. Stone Age hunters created them about six thousand years ago.

WINDHOEK The capital of Namibia features many buildings from the time when Namibia was a German colony. The imposing Alte Feste was designed as a fortress in 1890 and holds a museum. Windhoek also has a Zoo Park, a brewery, and traditional old churches, including Saint George's Cathedral and the Christuskirche.

apartheid: the policy of separate homes, schools, services, and neighborhoods for different ethnic groups, established in South Africa in 1948 and extended to Namibia when it was under the control of the South African government. Apartheid was outlawed in the early 1990s.

Baster: a person of mixed racial heritage who settled the area around Rehoboth in the nineteenth century and who survived as a distinct social group in modern Namibia

Benguela Current: a cold underwater current that runs from south to north off the Atlantic coast of Namibia

braai: an open fire barbecue, popular throughout Namibia

Bushveld: a savanna (grassland) region of northern Namibia. It receives the highest rainfall in the country.

communal land: an area held and controlled by local councils and township administrations. Communal land can be leased but cannot be owned by individuals.

gross domestic product (GDP): a measure of the total value of goods and services produced within the boundaries of a country in a certain amount of time (usually one year), regardless of the citizenship of the producers

inselberg: an "island mountain"; the name for isolated peaks that rise from the floor of Namibia's dry plains and desert regions

monsoon: a strong wind that blows across the Indian Ocean and southern Asia, often bringing heavy rains

native area: a region set aside for the use of certain ethnic groups when Namibia was governed as a province of South Africa. The native areas included Bushmanland, Ovamboland, Hereroland, and Damaraland.

okuruo: a community fire that the Herero believe allows them to communicate with spirits or ancestors

Oorlam: Khoisan-speaking groups that crossed into Namibia from South Africa and carried out raids on colonial farms and towns

Schutztruppe: German soldiers sent from Europe in the late 1800s and early 1900s to defend colonists' control of German Southwest Africa

seganpure: a long, one-stringed musical instrument created by the San people

Sperrgebiet: "forbidden zone"; an area closed to outside visitors that contains Namibia's largest field of rough diamonds

SWAPO: South West Africa People's Organization, the group formed in the 1960s to fight for the independence of Namibia from the control of South Africa

township: an area reserved for settlement by black African groups on the outskirts of large towns and cities

tribute: money or goods paid to a ruler

Selected Bibliography

CIA. *The World Factbook: Namibia*. 2007.
https://www.cia.gov/library/publications/the-world-factbook/geos/wa.html
(October 15, 2007).
This source offers statistics and background information on Namibia's economy, history, demographics, and more.

Cocker, Mark. *Rivers of Blood, Rivers of Gold: Europe's Conflict with Tribal Peoples*. London: Jonathan Cape, 1998.
This book describes the encounter of European colonialists and tribal societies. Included is a section on the clash between German colonists and black Namibians.

Gordon, Robert J. *The Bushman Myth: The Making of a Namibian Underclass*. Boulder, CO: Westview Press, 2000.
The author explains the role played by the San people in the struggle for independence and also as a familiar symbol of a bygone historical era in southern Africa.

International Defence and Aid Fund. *Namibia: The Facts*. London: IDAF Publications, 1989.
This short paperback book gives a general outline of Namibian society on the eve of independence.

Katjavivi, P. H. *A History of Resistance in Namibia*. London: James Curry, 1988.
An insider details the years of conflict in Namibia before independence. Katjavivi is a respected historian and was elected to the Constituent Assembly that drafted the new Namibian constitution.

Leys, Colin, and Susan Brown, eds. *Histories of Namibia: Living through the Liberation Struggle*. London: Merlin Press, 2004.
This series of oral histories presents ten Namibians who tell their stories through the violent years of the fight for independence from South Africa.

Namibia News. 2007.
http://namibianews.com (October 15, 2007).
This site offers the latest news about Namibian people, politics, sports teams, weather, and much more.

Population Reference Bureau. "2007 World Population Data Sheet." *Population Reference Bureau (PRB)*. 2007.
http://www.prb.org/pdf07/07WPDS_Eng.pdf (October 15, 2007).
This annual statistics sheet provides a wealth of data on Namibia's population, including rates of birth, death, fertility, and infant mortality, and other useful demographic information.

Reader, John. *Africa: A Biography of the Continent*. New York: Penguin Books, 1997.
The author offers a detailed overview of African history, from the earliest evidence of human settlement to the twentieth century. This book helps the reader understand Namibia's history in a wider context.

Sparks, Donald L. *Namibia: The Nation after Independence.* Boulder, CO: Westview Press, 1992.
The author details the transition to independence and describes the new government of Namibia and how it begins a gradual change in Namibia's economic systems.

Williams, Lizzie. *Footprint: Namibia.* 4th ed. Bath, UK: Footprint Handbooks, 2006.
This up-to-date traveler's guide to the country offers advice on how visitors can enjoy its culture and sights.

Campion, David. *Where Fire Speaks: A Visit with the Himba.* **Vancouver, BC: Arsenal Pulp Press, 2003.**
A journalist describes his stay with the Himba people of northern Namibia, who are struggling with the advance of modern civilization into their lands and traditional lifestyle.

Captsick, Peter H. *Sands of Silence: On Safari in Namibia.* **New York: St. Martin's Press, 1991.**
An experienced game warden and hunter describes a safari in the Kalahari Desert, where he tracks old bull elephants and other game and encounters the San, who still live a hunter-gatherer lifestyle.

Cornell, Kari A. *Cooking the Southern Africa Way.* **Minneapolis: Lerner Publications Company, 2005.**
Part of the Easy Menu Ethnic Cookbooks series, this recipe book introduces readers to the foods of Namibia and its neighbors.

Dawson, Jeff. *Dead Reckoning: The Dunedin Star Disaster.* **London: Orion Books, 2006.**
This book tells the story of a shipwreck of a British ship in 1942 off the Skeleton Coast of Namibia. Sixty-three people swam ashore from the ship only to find themselves struggling to survive in a barren desert.

Finley, Carol. *The Art of African Masks.* **Minneapolis: Lerner Publications Company, 1998.**
This book explores African civilizations through fascinating mask art.

Government of Namibia
http://www.grnnet.gov.na/
The official website of the Republic of Namibia offers pages on Our Government, Business and Industry, Foreign Relations, and "Namibia in a Nutshell."

Hamilton, Janice. *South Africa in Pictures.* **Minneapolis: Lerner Publications Company, 2004.**
South Africa's entry into the Visual Geography Series® covers the land, people, culture, and history of Namibia's southern neighbor.

Isaacson, Rupert. *The Healing Land: The Bushmen of the Kalahari.* **Boston: Grove Press, 2004.**
The author describes the many social and economic changes that have come to the San, one of the last hunger-gatherer societies on Earth.

Koppes, Steven. *Killer Rocks from Outer Space.* **Minneapolis: Twenty-First Century Books, 2004.**
A journalist looks at the evidence of killer rocks hitting Earth in the past and in the future.

Martin, Henno. *Sheltering Desert.* **London: William Kimber, 1957.**
The author describes the lives of two German scientists who took shelter from World War II in a remote Namibian canyon.

Further Reading and Websites

Namibia Nature Foundation
http://www.nnf.org.na/

This nonprofit group is dedicated to the preservation of Namibia's habitat and wildlife.

Namibia Tourism Board
http://www.namibiatourism.com.na/

This online guide to the country has sections on its people, politics, economy, and geography, a photo gallery, and list of tourist facilities, and links to other websites of interest.

The New York Times on the Web
http://www.nytimes.com

This online version of the newspaper offers current news stories along with an archive of articles on Namibia.

Parker, Linda. *The San of Africa*. Minneapolis: Lerner Publications Company, 2002.

In this account of the San, the author covers the history and culture of these nomadic peoples as they're forced to live in a society that is very different from the one they've always known.

Schoeman, Amy. *The Skeleton Coast*. Cape Town: Southern Book Publishers, 1986.

This book features a description of the harsh Skeleton Coast region in words and photographs.

Shostak, Marjorie. *Nisa: The Life and Words of a !Kung Woman*. Cambridge, MA: Harvard University Press, 2000.

An anthropologist from the United States meets a woman of the !Kung society and records her story. The book gives an interesting look at how traditional African peoples deal with life's many problems and setbacks in their own way.

Van der Post, Laurens. *The Lost World of the Kalahari*. Fort Washington, PA: Harvest Books, 1977.

The author vividly describes the Kalahari Desert and his encounters with the San living in the desert and following traditional customs.

vgsbooks.com
http://www.vgsbooks.com

Visit vgsbooks.com, the home page of the Visual Geography Series®. You can get linked to all sorts of useful online information, including geographical, historical, demographic, cultural, and economic websites. The vgsbooks.com site is a great resource for late-breaking news and statistics.

Zuehlke, Jeffrey. *Germany in Pictures*. Minneapolis: Twenty-First Century Books, 2002.

Germany's entry into the Visual Geography Series® covers the land, people, culture, and history of this European country that once controlled Namibia.

Captions for photos appearing on cover and chapter openers:

Cover: Kokerbooms, also known as quiver trees, are a type of aloe plant found naturally in Namibia and South Africa.

pp. 4–5 Windhoek, the capital of Namibia, enjoyed a generally peaceful transition from colonial rule to independence. Its modern buildings and streets are home to many different ethnic groups.

pp. 8–9 The Atlantic Ocean provides a stark contrast to the sand dunes of the Skeleton Coast near the port of Walvis Bay.

pp. 20–21 The rock paintings at Twyfelfontein in northwestern Namibia are the largest concentration of ancient art in Africa. They date from the late Stone Age (10,000–3,000 B.C.).

pp. 36–37 A group of schoolchildren pose for a picture in Ovamboland, a region just south of the Angola border.

pp. 46–47 Sellers display handmade goods at a market in north central Namibia.

pp. 56–57 Walvis Bay is a natural deepwater port, making it an important stopping place for ships and goods.

Photo Acknowledgments

The images in this book are used with the permission of: © Tibor Bognar/Alamy, pp. 4-5; © XNR Productions, pp. 6, 10; © Michael & Patricia Fogden/Minden Pictures/Getty Images, pp. 8-9; © Eric Nathan/Alamy, p. 12; © Fred Mayer/ Hulton Archive/Getty Images, p. 14; © Christophe Courteau/TMC/SuperStock, pp. 15, 20-21; © Meeyoung Son/Alamy, p. 16; © Images of Africa Photobank/ Alamy, p. 18; AP Photo/Tim Wright, p. 23; © INTERPHOTO Pressebildagentur/ Alamy, p. 25 (top); © akg-images, pp. 25 (bottom), 27; © Mary Evans Picture Library/Alamy, p. 26; © Topical Press Agency/Hulton Archive/Getty Images, p. 28; © Alexander Joe/AFP/Getty Images, pp. 31, 62; AP Photo/Alwyn van Zyl, p. 33; © Steve Thomas/Panos Pictures, p. 35; © Peter Bennett/eyevine/ZUMA Press, pp. 36-37; © Loetscher Chlaus/Alamy, p. 38; © age fotostock/SuperStock, p. 39; © Sean Spraque/The Image Works, pp. 40, 43 (top), 44; © Yabb Arthus-Bertrand/CORBIS, p. 43 (bottom); © AfriPics.com/Alamy, pp. 46-47; © iStock-photo.com, p. 48; © Trygve Bolstaed/Panos Pictures, p. 49; AP Photo/Michel Spingler, p. 52; © Frans Lemmens/zefa/CORBIS, pp. 56-57; © Blake Little/ The Image Bank/Getty Images, p. 58; © Bert Crawshaw/Art Directors, p. 60; © Wilmar Photography/Alamy, p. 64; Audrius Tomonis-www.banknotes.com, p. 68; © Laura Westlund/Independent Picture Service, p. 69.

Front cover: © Tom Till/Stone/Getty Images. Back cover: NASA.